THIS BOOK BELONGS TO

ooooooooooooooooooooo

TURTLE

Did you know...?

Turtles cry but not because they feel sad. Turtles' cry is simply part of "washing" eyes that are very important to these animals. Therefore, if we see a crying turtle, we already know that we do not have to feel sorry for him.

TURTLE

Did you know...?

In the case of leatherback turtles, we are dealing with an animal that is really huge – adults reach 400 kg of weight! The heaviest officially weighed specimen was 700 kg. It's like a small cow! Their length can reach 2 meters, and the front fins have a span of up to 3 meters.

TURTLE

Did you know...?

THE TORTOISE SHELL IS PART OF ITS SKELETON AND GROWS WITH IT. JUST LIKE OUR BONES!

TURTLE

Did you know...?

Turtles have a sensitive sense of smell that helps them find food. Perfect hearing helps them to hear potential threats. Great eyesight and color distinguishing. Turtles also have a very sensitive sense of touch. It is so sharp mainly for defensive reasons. When an animal feels that something is touching it, it can very quickly hide in its shell.

CHAMELEON

Did you know...?

CHAMELEONS LIVE AMONG THE LEAVES AND BRANCHES OF TREES, NATURE HAS ADAPTED THEM TO THIS, EQUIPPING THEIR PAWS WITH CLAWS THAT ENABLE THEM TO CLIMB AND EFFICIENTLY WANDER THROUGH THE FOREST.

CHAMELEON

Did you know...?

Chameleons do not change their body color depending on the color of their surrounding. Their coloration depends on the mood, state of health and emotions. Changing color is also a popular way to communicate with other animals. The intensity of the colors also depends on the surrounding temperature.

CHAMELEON

Did you know…?

THE EYES OF CHAMELEONS ARE INDEPENDENT OF EACH OTHER, SO EACH EYE CAN LOOK IN A DIFFERENT DIRECTION. THANKS TO THIS SKILL, CHAMELEON CAN OBSERVE ITS SURROUNDINGS WITHOUT TURNING ITS HEAD.

SNAKE

Did you know...?

SNAKES DO NOT HIBERNATE IN COLD CLIMATES. INTERESTINGLY, THEY FREEZE IN THE COLD. THEY ARE STILL CONSCIOUS BUT INACTIVE.

SNAKE

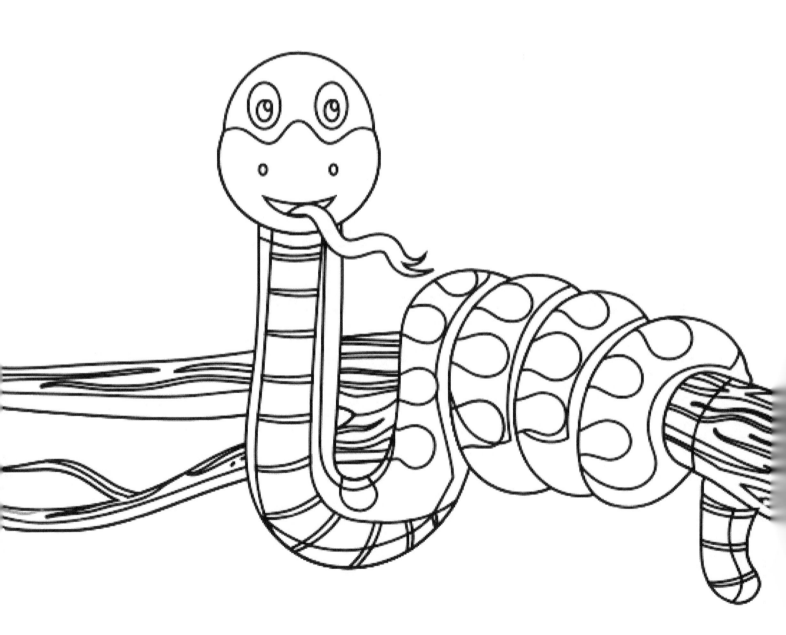

Did you know...?

SNAKES HAVE FORKED TONGUES THAT ALLOW THEM TO DETERMINE THE DIRECTION FROM WHICH THE SCENT IS COMING. SNAKES ARE DEAF AND HAVE POOR EYESIGHT. THEY ONLY FEEL SOUND VIBRATIONS.

SNAKE

Did you know…?

The king cobra is the largest poisonous snake in the world, reaching less than six meters in length and weighing up to nine kilograms. It is mainly found in southern China, Indochina, Malaysia and the Philippines. Adults can live up to thirty years.

CROCODILE

Did you know...?

Some crocodiles can live very long. The oldest ones live up to 75 years old, so they may be older than humans.

CROCODILE

Did you know...?

Crocodiles have the strongest bite of any animal in the world. However, the muscles that open the jaws of crocodiles are not that strong. An adult person can keep the crocodile's jaw closed with their bare hands.

ALLIGATOR

Did you know...?

ALLIGATORS ARE MASSIVE ANIMALS THAT CAN WEIGH OVER 400 KILOGRAMS AND BE 3 TO 4 METERS LONG.

ALLIGATOR

Did you know...?

As soon as the little alligators are born, they can go and grab their own food. Young American alligators are approximately 15 to 20 cm long. After about two years, they leave their mother to start their own families.

LIZARD

Did you know…?

Most lizards have suction cups on their legs that enable them to climb up vertical slippery surfaces. They have exceptionally good eyesight, and some can see colors in sharp focus.

LIZARD

Did you know...?

Lizards smell things with their tongues. Like snakes, the lizard sticks out its tongue to catch scent particles in the air, then pulls its tongue back and places these particles at the top of its mouth where special sensory cells are located.

WELL DONE!

Printed in the USA
CPSIA information can be obtained
at www.ICGtesting.com
LVHW062300281124
797908LV00038B/1482